New Issues Poetry & Prose

Editor	Herbert Scott
Copy Editor	Lisa Lishman
Managing Editor	Marianne E. Swierenga
Assistants to the Editor	Rebecca Beech, Christine Byks
Fiscal Officer	Marilyn Rowe

New Issues Poetry & Prose
The College of Arts and Sciences
Western Michigan University
Kalamazoo, MI 49008

First Edition, 2005.

ISBN   1-930974-49-3
Library of Congress Cataloging-in-Publication Data:
Boyle, Kevin
A Home for Wayward Girls/Kevin Boyle
Library of Congress Control Number: 2004116687

Art Director	Tricia Hennessy
Designer	Emily Butkus
Production Manager	Paul Sizer
	The Design Center
	School of Art
	College of Fine Arts
	Western Michigan University

for MARGARET –
thanks + I hope
–you enjoy it –
Best of luck
Kevin
Boyle
7/11/06
S.C. CA.

A HOME FOR
WAYWARD
GIRLS

KEVIN BOYLE

New Issues

 WESTERN MICHIGAN UNIVERSITY

For my parents—
Bernard and Margaret

For my brothers and sisters—
Margaret Mary, Brian, Patricia, John and Kathleen

For my daughters—
Tess and Marina

And, especially, for my wife—
Cassie

Contents

Acknowledgments

Alaska Quarterly Review: "The Gods' Breasts"

Antioch Review: "Getting Clean"

Blackbird: "Legerdemain"

Charlotte Poetry Review: "Writing the Body"

Cottonwood: "Going Back," "Romeo Bound," "Near Lissadell"

Colorado Review: "Family"

Delmar: "Death of the Drama Poem"

Denver Quarterly: "Catechize"

Fan Magazine: "Lucky Kid"

Greensboro Review: "What History Joined Together," "The Visible"

Interim: "Stamped by Harvard's Literary Society, The Signet"

Michigan Quarterly Review: "Through Science"

Natural Bridge: "Begetter and Begotten"

North American Review: "Before Bed," "In Heat," "Oneness," "Unhitched"

Northwest Review: "Beyond the Pleasure Principle," "Excision," "Masturbating on Ash Wednesday," "The Heart of It"

Passages North: "The Consumers," "Still Life, *Nature Morte*"

Pavement: "Losing Myself"

Poet Lore: "Recall," "Above Tree Line"

Poetry East: "The Lullaby of History"

Shade: "Permanent Collection," "Our Last Child's First Day of School"

Southern Poetry Review: "The Church Universal"

storySouth: "Predilection," "Waking," "Wayward Girls"

"Through Science" was republished in the *1997 Anthology of Magazine Verse and Yearbook of American Poetry.*

"The Visible" won the *Greensboro Review* Poetry Award in 1999. Some of these poems appeared in my chapbook, *The Lullaby of History,* which won the North Carolina Writers' Network Mary Belle Campbell Poetry Prize.

"The Lullaby of History" also appears in *The Book of Irish American Poetry from the Eighteenth Century to the Present,* Daniel Tobin (editor), University of Notre Dame Press (2005).

Thanks to so many people who helped me in the writing of these poems. In particular I'd like to thank Steve Collins, David Ogden, Carole Dragone, Margaret Mary Boyle, Bill Zaranka, Joel Conarroe, Stephen Dobyns, Michael Chadwick, Kristen Catalano, Jorie Graham, Linda Gregg, Kyle Torke, Edward Hirsch, Don Eron, Stuart Dischell and Agha Shahid Ali. Thanks also to Elon University for a sabbatical—time away from teaching—and for allowing me to teach what I love. And, finally, thanks to my closest reader, Cassie Kircher.

I.

The Lullaby of History

I put the bookmark in the page after Lincoln's
silence during the 1860 campaign, after no one
in the Gulf States cast a single vote for him,
then march off to the car, carseat in tow, drive on
cruise, mainly, to the site in Durham where Sherman
coaxed the Southern general—Johnston—
to submit twice, sign twice. The six hundred thousand
dead were like the shucks inside the reconstructed
bed, the smoke the chimney slewed, the clayish mud.
In the museum, name-tagged women watch our daughter,
four months here, while we investigate the flags
with gunshot holes, the uniforms with gunshot holes,
the shells of the Union Army with three rings, the shells
of the Confederate's with two. We take our daughter
to the filmstrip, where she sleeps through
the stills of uniformed corpses in ditches and cries
at war's end, one flag for all these states. We ride,
strapped, to the Greek restaurant known for its sauces
and lamb, stroll inside the tobacco warehouse transformed
into a mall, each glass pane so large a truck
could drive through and pick up brightleaf to ship.
They say this section profited when South met North
and troops took in the smoke of this leaf, spreading
by word of mouth the flavor, until the profits
were so large owners began to donate. In the antique store
we happen upon a map my father might love
of Ireland before division, just as it appeared
when he was born, the north a section, not another country,
Ulster's counties awash in the orange the mapmakers
stained it. But we can't commit to buy for this price,
or prevent our daughter from falling asleep as we discuss
facts the map makes clear: battles marked in bold,
our side losing again and again, the Flight of the Earls,
Vinegar Hill, the Battle of the Boyne, and we donate

9

a moment during the drive home to feel
the weight of the centuries' dead, almost cry for all
those men who gave their skin to the ground so young,
so young brought their lips to earth and let their mouths
cave in, accept the soil as their voice. We did not wake
our girl through this. *Let her sleep,* we said.

Predilection

Not the high jinks of men haltered to limbs
buzzing the hickory down, but the sawdust
left for mulch by the stump the red ants
stream across, rouge on the pale wood.
Not the pool drained of kids during the storm
that passes miles away, but the jockstrap
left after five that the stall washer finds,
a name clearly sewn in the elastic.
Not the linden in bloom but its fragrance
overtaken by the cloud of Nissan exhaust.
Not the original of anything, but the "preowned,"
the hand-me-downs and rags of dolls,
their limbs or eyes left in other towns,
in the laundromat where the poor watch
their clothes fray in the cool-down cycle
or rinse. Not the broken-bat double bringing
the runner in from first, but the line in the stadium john,
the two men pissing into the fountain for washing up,
and the antennas bent by the boys watching your car,
then broken for swords and dropped. Not the music
you make love alongside of, the sexual appetites
so keen your jaw is loose, but this duet for
spare change these slightly rancid men pitch your way.
Not the umbilical cord severed, just the knife
and the sewing up after the baby passes through.
Not your hand but the man's electric hand-held massage
pushing into her neck and shoulders, her bra strap
loose at the end, her eyes glassy when she tips him.
Not the sea but the salt and sand buckled under the waves.
Not the opening of the windows to put the screens in,
but the flagstone steps leading you to the headstone rows.
Not the aspen, but the rake, the pile and the burning.

11

Romeo Bound

—for Michael and Elise

With my head as rich as swill, the one-night tattoo
stamped near my wrist now a smeared blue code,
I wanted more to drink after closing. One happy, thin,
black woman, loaded, her voice an octave above
my thoughts, asked me to the after-hours club
I knew was for blacks only. The town is simple
as a triangle, really: Hispanics own the hollow toward
the tracks, blacks cover the streets from Highland
to the river in a slope, and whites plot the high ground
to the east. If it is early and you are careful or
if it is late and you are drunk, you can go anywhere
and feel safe. So, happy to dance after drinking,
my feet skidding along the wet passing stripes
down the center of the street, I went with her.
After drinking a boilermaker round, we danced
inside some pop funk first, then some slow things,
an exchange of bodies in our hands. Maybe there are
a few things better than being empty-headed,
with an erection, in danger, and a woman
in your arms. Nothing more than my chest touched
her breasts, I did not kiss even her forehead or cheeks,
I did not hold her hands or even say much over
the clatter except, "I got to go to the toilet," and left her
at the bar drinking. Joining me in the men's room
were three guys who said, "Get the fuck out of here"
over and over, while one held my lips at knife-point
and another pissed on my pants and shoes.
I hurried through a goodbye at the bar and saw her
again once, a while back, on lunch at Sal's Sub Shop.
She was beautiful in the day and sober, and we spoke:
"Keeping dry these days?" she said. I said, "Yeah,"
and that was that. She smiled and ate in one spot
of the room, and I took mine outside into fall.

Autumn is something in Ossining: the palisade
so grounded, the leaves dying, the prison, the tugs' labor.
From the hill I could see the width of river and spit
gristle onto the grass around the town's bank clock.

Stamped By Harvard's Literary Society, The Signet

I entered with my own key to the deep chairs downstairs,
a huge waiting room for nowhere with coffee-tabled magazines
I spread like a fortuneteller's cards that said,
"Today you will become another man." I was the handyman
with abilities in oiling the chairs' leather, in turning
brushes against the toilet rims' rust, or forcing
the urine drops with a cleanser that turned
from white to blue. I knew the first thing about tinkering
with the toilet's inner life, adjusting the floating ballcock
so that its copper shine, as it rose and rose, would suddenly

shut every gate of moisture and keep the bowl silent
and ready. I had table legs to grease and bend
until the next time I would unbend them and dress the tables.
I pinched pennies into window frames to keep the wind
from knocking and Windexed windows so those who passed
could witness my cleanliness. For lunch, I was given leftover
gala Harvard food by my boss and was allowed to read
the books stamped SIGNET and autographed by Harvard authors
after I walked my vacuum across the longest Oriental rug
and dusted with a feather duster I recognized not from life
but a porno-magazine feature on a woman cleaning house
in heels and lipstick and a fanfare of color—a duster guarding
faultily her private parts gone public for my once adolescent
lust. She was not paid what it was worth to me then.

My boss was British with four American sons, a bright,
exhausted woman, a caretaker who was always kind to me.
One day, as I smacked the straight broom's handle into
my palm, we talked about how she ended up with the small room
I did not clean and her odd job, how she had
once herself written a book called *My Father,*
Bertrand Russell. Back at work, I swept the long hall

lined with yearbooks and football pennants, went past
the six-foot-tall window's sun and through the dark
of the paneled walls, not thinking. And then, as if
in a comic strip, I knocked the wood of the handle against
my noggin and said, "You idiot," and spoke with her before
the bike trip home, and read the book, and worked thereafter
with an uneasiness. I thought I had been paying my
juvenile dues, had expected this job to blossom one day
into some sprawling piece of luck, with my hand
waving to someone beneath the trees, a wife or child
at the end of the drive returning almost happily to me.

But here she was, gifted, a pseudo-boss, in her fifties,
the daughter of nobility in fact, an actual dame,
and seemingly poor, having failed at the one event she thought
she—unlike her father—could master: love and family.
I couldn't explain then my fascination with her:
divorced, sad in some appropriate way, generous and shy,
she was someone for whom I felt neither passion nor love,
but someone in whom I saw the possibilities
for life's failures. When I finally stepped up to
an easier job and more hours driving for Clinical Data,
I kissed her, my one brush with nobility, and stole
an autographed book by Robert Bly dedicated to the Signet
in which Spanish snow fell, and souls left bodies almost
and farms woke in flower or lay fallow—it didn't matter.

Permanent Collection

If Rembrandt had dieted more and eaten lean, and perhaps only
white meat, then gelled his hair and shaved
his little mouse-face hairs, then had his colors done
—a bit more red, maybe auburn or rust—
instead of that dumpy brown, with a cork-colored wall behind him
—imagine it with flowers (hyacinths plus crocuses for *printemps*)—
and if he learned to smile—genuine too, not just for the camera
which was his eye, no, something to pierce you—
and if he didn't have those belabored eyes, those sad-sack eyes,
imagine how he could get on in the world
we inhabit, where I for one look pretty good, all right, great—24/7—,
and if I didn't I'd call 911, or 999
at our London home, where we go to theatre almost biweekly,
seeing the best look their best on stage, the buxom young ones who
    can
remember so many lines, and the measurements of that one—
88-60-92—who, it was said, "rose above the standard of perfection,"
oh metric world in which I perhaps would not fit.
And when I give my weight in stone, I feel so paltry,
nary-a-man, so narrow and contained,
I can barely say it—13 stone—
there it is. My unluck: my workouts without stop have come
to that: 13 stone. But at home where bombs will be bombs,
I feel really good, I mean almost fantastic, with numbers that MAKE
SENSE, and not kilometers to go before I sleep etc.
Oh art world I love, your openings that open my eyes to this world
we see and without which we would not see quite so well,
how I enjoy you, and covet more EUROS with which to buy you
to make me more spiritual, more head over heels in love with
this LIFE. But let's not forget the REAL, the stuff that will fade and
    crumble
(I suppose it all will, come firestorm, come firebomb),
even Eva Maria Gonzalez, *la nueva* MISS ESPAÑA, what looks!

The way that sash
moves out and then in as if in a breeze, the fullness
of the E and S, and that inhale on the final ÑA,
and the pearls, the plucked brows and nose,
the deforestation of her underarms and French-cut
bikini line. Let's not go there. This is the place
to get off and disembark, alighting not in some foreign local,
but a home of sorts, a thinking man's rest stop
with healthful options.

Losing Myself

In the Sears aisles of hedge trimmers, welders, Frigidaires and key-
    makers,
I studied the sucking pull of freezer doors,
fingered the oiled joints of garden shears, listened
to my father's hand wrestle his pocket change to a decision.
I made pretend
my tongue could talk as fast as the third speed of fans,
my father's going to work was the electric burner turning from black
    to red to black to red to black to red coils,
and my stomach was the Hoover bag.
I touched my fingers into my father's belt loops
when they spoke of rules for rip starting the mowers, mounting the
    jigsaw, planing the oak boards true,
and I listened to the intricate unhinged whir of machines I knew could
    fly outside this world.
But only the small, hand-controlled electric clipper my father bought
scared me with its different heads for butch or massage.
What science we walked through together for our rung-up sales.

Maybe I shopped with my mother when I was younger,
but I always roamed, except from outside the dressing rooms where I
    could hear
the static lifting from dresses going over their heads
like sparks running off the wards of keys being grooved.
She couldn't control my losing spells or wanted to
find me in the dark she could pull me from, scolding
with her hand in my hair, talking in the future tense about my father
    hearing.
So I ran to the bins that sold dull clothes
folded into piles of sports shirts and slacks that could be thumbed
    through,
but beneath these, inside the slide-back door, were the clothes I
    believed in,
that were like earth to fall in

and close myself from light, tiles, the bodies, sales,
and rock my head into my knees, everything muffled
in the smell of Sears clothes, everything
held outside the thin slat of light I almost never sealed out
      completely,
letting it be a line of Indian headdress, or a healing scar from
      my face's tip to chin.
Then I rocked until I swayed and dizzied myself and hoped
my mother's calves would soon show up above her shoes
      pointing toward me,
accusing leather, rule-making shins, and balls of knees to stare
      at me like a strict column of bone.
Her hands found me out and lifted me above the bins
toward the high, high ceilings,
and then her voice, my head trying to rest into her skirt,
      between her legs, and her hand through and through my
      hair.
*Don't get lost again now. We have to get home now. You don't
      want Daddy to know, do you?*

But I always found my way back, or buried myself in rows
of coat racks, warmed myself in the smell of black leathers,
hiding my feet in scarves, muffs, rain hats, or dress clothes,
or at home when everyone older worked the chores on Saturday
      mornings,
I'd sit in the closed closet behind the eight coats where the
      vacuum should be,
where the attachments usually sprawled across their nails,
and in the absence of uprights and plugs
I'd rock on Kathleen's yellow jacket I loved until I dizzied myself
and waited for someone's hands to shrill the hangers across the
      coat bar
and show my hair riding down and up, waited for her hands
to call me out, for her to say,

19

Kevin, we all have our chores to do, her hands
all over my head that still soared like an appliance let loose,
my head still nodding and saying,
Yes, Mom, yes, Mom, yes, Mom, yes, Mom, yes, Mom.

Lucky Kid

—for Don

I was lucky when I was eleven
in my good shorts and Philly's heat,
my sneaks scuffed out from pitching
halfballs on concrete, my belly
swollen from the cupped hands of water
taken from the outside spigot
too often again. My mom still
filing through her day's work, my father
away at reserves for the week. My sisters
maybe ironing in the basement, damping
their shirts and mine with a shake
of water from the used Coke bottle,
then rolling them neatly into lines
of heavy cotton loaves,
or sitting for a neighbor's kids
while she had her hair done under
a hive of heat. My brothers doing work
with their arms I admired, lifting
mowers onto the rusted beds of trucks,
busing trays in a hospital lunch room,
or just sitting on a bed in our attic
paging slowly through a *Playboy*
they bought or found by the tracks,
rained on but still good.

But I was lucky
because the heart of the house
was mine with only one chore listed
under my name for the day. No one but me
would touch the laundered slip covers,
the polished wood of the dining room table,
the pulled-back curtains, or the sacred bones,
our relics of a genuine saint. So in my sweat,

my T-shirt stained at the sleeves from
keeping my face clean, I did my vacuuming
of the living room rug, kicked around
the fat legs of the dining room chairs,
looking for the crumbs only a parent
could see, and then just stood
that vacuum at ninety degrees and let it
hum. And I lay on a cool patch of floor
where the sun hadn't been, listening to
the noise, and didn't think
of any one of us gone for good, just waited
till my mind eased up like a halfball caught
in a breeze that wouldn't give in, and I
went through all the rules I knew for
wireball, stepball, halfball and touch,
and arrived at the facts I was born to:
I was the last of six kids, the son of
an immigrant on a street of accented tongues,
a Catholic on a block of Sunday Catholics,
and I owned that place, from the highest
telephone pole wires to the sewers
we raked things from.

Wayward Girls

—for Steve

It must have been a corporal work of mercy, akin
to visiting the sick or burying the dead, our visit
to the Home for Wayward Girls, a busload of us taken
away from our thoughts of girls to girls ridiculously
uniformed in dresses their bodies made their own.
We didn't cast lots, but I turned away from my back-
of-the-bus group to slow dance with a girl so wayward
I felt my head slip from resting against her hair and
I began to speak in tongues with her, quietly, the gist
of the Holy Ghost upon us, she brushing so much of her body
against mine I thought my good suit would catch fire.
"Slow down," she repeated. "Dance like the niggers dance."
I imitated that bend of the body, the swish of leg
into dress, the close press of my right hand sifting
dress and buttock skin through it, my chest joining
the draw of her chest, and over punch, during the two
fast songs we stood still through to find ourselves again,
she spoke of nothing but music, no hint of abandonment or abuse.
During the last dance, as the DJ said, "Last dance before
the bus leaves, before you're back in bed," she said,
as she lifted her lips away from my neck and its tattoo
for the morning, "You're not half bad. Come back again."
I looked her almost in the eye, imagined myself palming
her head and stroking her neck-long hair she said they cut
to size, and with my hands at my side said, "I'd like that."
In the bus windows we could see ourselves, altar boys
returning to the rigors of discipline, our looks groomed
the way we edged our lawns or whipped the dogs who let
loose, and over the bad mike at the front of the bus,
the priest said, "God will bless you for your kindness.
Remember them, boys, in your prayers."

23

The Church Universal

At weekday mass in summer, the nuns' veils held
a layered, synthetic aroma, something that walked

beside them and joined the sounds of their beads
swinging against their thighs, and as they knelt

at the communion rail, closed their eyes and opened
their mouths, exposing the work of laymen in silver

and gold, I'd breathe in their bodies, attentive to
the communion plate I held beneath their tongues, sometimes

accidentally touching their necks' skin, and the plate
would reveal, as I passed from mouth to mouth, the smallest

hints of host, the smallest crumbs that fell from
their lips, uncolored like men's lips. The priest

would later, at the altar, with his thumbs and index fingers,
brush and coax the pieces of God into his chalice

and swirl his wine to meet them, and drink, mixing his mouth
with theirs. Afterwards the priest would undress

before me, and I would help with his cincture and alb,
and the nuns would cross the street in groups, and I

would receive the blessing on my knees and ride my bike home,
my cassock and surplice, on a hanger, sending a plume

behind me, a bright train. In the kitchen my grandmother
would already have the bacon—sliced in small pieces—

cooking, and when the cassock hanger scraped the closet
rung, I would hear the eggs get fork-scrambled

in her glass bowl and join the bacon in the frying pan.
I remember most her pleasure as she sat by the kitchen window

and began her day watching the children in the drive,
the cars returning and leaving, the blinds rising

and falling, and she'd turn to me from time to time
and smile, almost mischievously, certainly pridefully,

knowing I loved what she had given, that I cleaned the plate
with the bread, taking in the last stains of yolk and grease.

Writing The Body

In New York, watching with amazement the wealthy
thumbing *The Times* in plastic
gloves for protection, I remembered the now
dead paper in Philadelphia I once delivered for,
and my first day on the job that summer
with my red hand-me-down
Schwinn's frame ready to hold
as I balanced the sixty-some
between my legs in the pure
white Bulletin Bag they awarded you
for a dollar something. Inside the paper-branch shed,
across from Joe's Home Plate Grill
where I'd eventually waste
my disposable income, beside the ruined car
lot, I was welcomed into the union
of boys principally by Sullivan, the branch manager, his face
damaged by a gene pool, and at seventeen our leader.
He ordered me to sit on three uncut bundles
in the center of the room, a king
with a rebellious court. I sat
my life still, an initiate. I sat for the artist in them
and their skills with the pen: They magic-
markered me up with their thoughts and musings about
my mother's semi-private parts (while she worked at the Navy Depot,
filling requests for nuts and bolts to keep our troops safe in
Da Nang) or they spoke to the race question,
or commented generally on the procreant urge.
One, not without skill in drawing,
placed a huge penis falling from my
shorts' pocket to my kneecap
and stuck a Cupid's arrow through its head.
Or they wrote on me that God Blows
or Jews Suck and then they stopped, arrested
not by fatigue or doubt but a completed canvas.

They autographed their initials into their
accomplishment and lifted me like a football
hero into the latched and windowless upstairs room
where the old papers got rained on and I sprawled in
the ink mess, headlines spreading, unable
to be read. Everything was gone in the dark.
Unlocked after three hours, I biked back
home, my grandmother scrubbed for a tabula rasa,
shaking her head, "Who could have done such a thing?"
Who would have thought that the next day
I would be just one more number—route 15—
among a set and not one
paperboy in the troop
would have an ax
to grind against me. I made the cut.
I was in. The money was OK for my grade
and this was what one did after altar boys—
a step up. I'm rising still.

II.

Getting Clean

Before even the willows were green
I took my week of vacation and drove alone
to the mountains five hours from town, and rode
immediately without a sound, no radio, no voice,
just breathing weeks out of me, the window
open for smelling leaf mold, smelling the dead
skunk's spray, smelling what my breath made.

I was soon happy without the complication of flowering trees,
happy in the color of rivers all around me:
in stone, in beech, black highway, mud bends of rivers.

But it wasn't until the third day of drinking nights,
fishing days, while sitting on a flat patch of rock,
casting at a new curve in the river, that I rested.
I went down the line finally and settled
on the bottom as I used to do as a boy, when my mind
could do such things often, when I was alone
enough to keep down there a long time.
Lying there, now emptied of history and of news,
not looking up the line but onto the river floor
of flush and dead life, I came into pleasure
which is winter, the whole thing scraped clean.
And I stayed like that for what I wanted
to be hours or the four remaining days,
and came up in a few minutes to my fishing rod
looking silly, all lacquered and raised toward the sky,
my bait living slowly inside the box.

I wrote then my letter to you,
explaining what I saw out the window that night
of no stars, and why I shook almost
as you won me back to bed, why I drift
even out the other side of sex back into myself,

and then wake in the mornings still touching you,
still wanting us to be two empty creatures
unable to get past the bottom of things.

The Visible

I suppose it's hard to begin reading Yeats
anywhere, but I began on the El, commuting
from my father's monastic site in the Northeast
to West Philadelphia's Ivy League ghetto.
As a hog for footnotes and fact, perhaps
more than music or image at the time—what music
more insistent, more dramatic than the El's,
what bodies more defined by the repetition
of wheel-grind into them—I read about
Hugh Lane's wanting to give an art collection
to Dublin if the city would only build a museum
to house it, and Yeats' worry that Ireland,
by rejecting Lane, would be a "huckstering nation,
groping for a halfpence in a greasy till
by the light of a holy candle." I recognized
myself in his worry: I was his Ireland
with my scapulas, the St. Blase candles wedged
against my throat in winter, the novenas for
our dead, and the supermarket I clerked in
for those five years, my till a shambles
with bills never stacked but always fantailing.
I read that Maud Gonne thought Hugh Lane
a social climber, "acting as after all
one expects a Jew picture dealer to do"
because he made his pounds in that world,
and all I could imagine was our Miriam
who worked Express and the Nazis' tattoo
she revealed as she bagged her certain way.
And I read Hugh Lane's aunt, Lady Gregory,
say, "These Dubliners don't work or get up early,
or take the trouble to keep themselves clean,
and yet they cry out against any who look from
things visible to things invisible." I ended up
siding with the enemy of Yeats, the prick Murphy—

who locked his workers out—because at least
he spoke a good line about building new digs
for the poor, rather than housing for Corot.

Even today, though I intuit what the invisible means
and provides, I still look toward the bodies
raising up pallets with the forklift, the wrist bands
for carpal tunnel by the bedside, the varicose
lines going toward the delta of the thighs
beneath the coats at the El stop, beneath
the dresses that rise as the clerks bend for
the dropped coin, the fallen coupon, the marbled
steak. As a face turns from the register toward
me—the customer—and the exchange, the lips announcing
a price, the hands accepting the transaction,
I remember those days of thirst, not necessarily
for something unseen, but for something fuller,
something better that was not just art.

Going Back

The dungarees were down to our thighs and things
were funny at the start, us laughing

at the sky, a circle of blue,
and the corn rows, a half-foot of stubble
going sight-wide up the hill. Our being opened
so clearly to November made those laughs,
with the four fields around us rising
into farmhouses that from a distance looked toward us.

The moon rose up, an imperfect man beyond
three-quarters full as we, on our backs, lifted
our pants back on.

If a combine rode by crazed with some football defeat,
we were doomed, sure
to be sucked in, our teeth
torn loose and pitched to the grain wagon behind, our bodies
only husks left to brown.
That was your idea. Mine was to have sex
with all the wired-in cows watching
as they worked their mouths.

The fields cleared, showing after months, probably
brought us to it. Or the rusted harrow
standing up as fence. Or the thick smell
of cowlife and soil. Or the milkweed seed
we coaxed into letting out early.
Or the talk about failure we drove out there for,
wanting out of the house, needing
a ride into something bigger.

Unhitched

The motel electricity shut down.
Doors opened. Mouths
Became neighborly. All walls went slim.
The fern in the hanger turned a blue, the space
Heater's last color was closest to rich cake, dark cake.
The Gideons became possessed
Of emendations and graffiti, the blanket
And your pubic hair felt mopey, pressed flat.
You knew something had changed and seahorsed
Closer to me, a curvature in your spine and mine.

I had seen the shaped rows of artichokes pointing to the sea
And the island beyond, between the two trawlers,
That grew artichokes the size of swollen knees.
Sprayers lapsed in a runnel, and a patch of oil
Where we stopped made a heart in the road.
I drove my foot through it, made feathers at one end,
A pretty, blunt, smudged tip at the other.
Then lay and measured my body against the passing stripe—
You were right! They're at least ten feet tall.
The sky had gone dark earlier so it was a surprise to no one
That around four the rains poured aslant toward Japan.
Holy heavens it stormed!
The signs that read Rock Slides prophesied.

I unbuttoned the button at your hip,
Drove on through the shenanigans of scree and wind,
My index finger washing around inside of you,
And drove with a straight face, an earnest face.

At the motel: The jingling of the keys, the rain condemning
The umbrellas of news that capped our heads, the lights shaping
Coronas from mist. You slept through the electric crisis
And the other language you talk in your sleep.

We were haphazardly glad, close
In the morning and made our type of love
Before the joys of Denny's chain breakfast number one.

Still Life, *Nature Morte*

While we leaf quietly through the Cezanne
that joins us near the hip, through
Still Life With Apples, Still Life With Onions,
Still Life With Peaches, we are so enamored of
the flesh and what it consumes that we begin to love—
even after all these years—the flesh of our thighs,
the hands that turn the page and last night held
the peaches—still hard—and cut the onions. The hands
still smell slightly when held beneath my nose
and our tongues that just lay there
and took the wine are up, riled, talking.
You turn the page onto *Still Life With Jugs* and we pun
on jugs, think in passing of the word "conjugal"
you played in Scrabble the night we were making up,
becoming whole bodies to ourselves again, our mouths
not just anger holes with teeth. And then we flip
to *Still Life With Skull, Skull and Candlestick,*
Three Skulls on an Oriental Rug, Pyramid of Skulls,
Skull on a Drapery, and finally *A Vase of Flowers.*
You remember and report back: Cezanne worked from paper
flowers, the living died too quickly. Life is short,
Art is slow, we joke and then head back, as if in review,
to *Still Life With Skull.* The skull lacks a lower jaw,
but it does have deep sockets, and a gaping nose hole
for air, or a thumb perhaps, reminding us of the nights
we used to bowl, but we couldn't master that. A pear stem
tickles the air where the ear should have been.
Another pear accepts plaudits for its beauty from the space
where the tongue once lay. The nearly circular fruit,
the cute, unsliced lime reminds you of the forms
the laparoscope saw inside you—a kind of marbled bocce ball
the photos showed, a veined, swollen shape.
We reflect on all the empty spaces we hold
within ourselves, our great potential for nothingness.

We see ourselves gone and admit the flesh can become
so unwieldy, so chaotic, so prone to decay that the hands,
the lips, even the voice rising from its box seem false,
so ephemeral that we would not touch them with a stick.

Through Science

After the progesterone and pergonal, the shots
in the buttocks, in the undersides of your arm,
left, then right, for weeks, day and night, after
the metrodine and stirrup probes, long after
the surgery through the navel—laparoscopy—
and the wound across your pubic hair—laparotomy—
let the doctor see the tubal occlusion magnified,
irreparable, after the long nights of making love
when we would rather have read or continued our fight
or slept, after the parents' ideas about God's love,
after everyone we knew had found themselves pregnant
with singletons and twins, after your good friend's
abortion of her fetus that did not come at a good time,
we, after all this time, waiting in the restaurant near
Christmas in Nebraska to hear the result from
the blood drawn, from the eggs retrieved and fertilized,
from the cannula inserted and the embryos let free
inside of you, heard the voice at the other end
say our number was high, science had triumphed. We cried,
surrounded by conversations from the lunchtime crowd,
saying nothing. And then for weeks talked with doctors
who monitored the high risks, who spoke of the chance
of miscarriage, who cautioned us to remain calm, and then
cautiously one placed the wand inside you at ten weeks,
and revealed on the screen this dark child whose heart—
it was nearly all heart—beat so quickly no one could
keep count—perhaps one hundred and eighty beats in
the minute we watched, and the next minute we watched,
and the next minute we watched. When this child is born,
when this child opens its eyes to the world of science
all around—the metal shine, the blood on the uniforms,
the blue masks and skin-toned gloves, the umbilical cord
cut with hygienic blades—I'll want this child to go quickly

to your breasts, to lie there and hear some song that rises
up through the sucking sounds, and to be so soothed by the taste
of you and the sounds of its own action that it will believe
in its own inevitability, its own delight in the senses,
its own place in this zone we try to bring spirit to.

The Gods' Breasts

In the breast-feeding video, Jan receives
from her partner two bags of frozen peas
she places on her engorged breasts, applies
them through the towel, the green vegetables
harmonizing nicely with the brown of towel
and loveseat. The lactation consultant
suggests cold cabbage leaves only twice a day
or tea bags applied to blistered nipples.
Remember, the milk comes through many holes
in the nipple, so be sure baby latches on
completely, sucks the whole areola in.
Spent, we drive home from class, you recalling
your Nebraskan pig litters, how sows would
bury their taxed nipples in mud slime,
how piglets would root around in the puddle
of slurred ground. I spoke of Greek myth,
my fresh fellow feeling for Diana and Athena,
without having even seen the C-section video.
Athena seems doubly shrewd in coaxing Hephaestus
to fashion a suit of armor to cover her
breasts and brawn, the payment being permission
granted for him to paw around, a godly slob
who wiggles some and comes on her leg. She dabs
her thigh with a rag she finds inside the forge,
and sends it packing down through the layers of
ether to lie on Gaea, earth mother, who gives birth
to Erectheus. Perhaps the gods were not mammals,
because you never hear of them holding Dionysus'
chilled grape leaves or Demeter's chilled peas
to their breasts. Nothing about our in-class learning:
shields, leaks at work, inverted nipples or hand pumps.
No, the little gods grow up in myth, some on nectar,
some on smoke from sacrificed ox, and although
one or two might slice at the testicles of
their dads with sharpened sickles, most manage.

They or their friends might be served in hot stews,
might need to appease winds with throat slashings,
or become transformed into myrtles, poplars,
a tree that bears fruit, but they do just fine.
Nowhere do we hear about the trials of nursing gods.
Perhaps a verse on the dugs of a she-wolf
as she suckles Rome's twins, but generally myth is
a good place to nurse the young without pain.

Id

We say, *Touch your ear, your ear,* and she
pokes her eye, rims a nostril. We write
the power-bill check for fifty odd, and she
walks it under the table, tears and eats.
At the chic restaurant she moves bowels
as if she were moving mountains, all muscle
and grimace. She calls from her crib—morning—
while we are making love, before my wife's
side of the exchange. I go to her and find her doll—
pink Nora—with four teeth around her neck;
then it falls a yard through the jail bars—pushed.
Lifted, she returns to the off-limits cabinet
again for her oil and flour; she drops pliers
on my knee as I handyman the childproofing
screw into what has the appearance of wood, but
yields like steel. She tosses pacifiers into
her demonstration potty, washes her hands in
adult toilet water, then licks, refreshed.
She's the genius of the house. First word:
banana. State bird: the stuffed cloth cockatiel
hanging on a string at her window; she leans
her face into it, admiring the outside, the home
of the moon she beams for, stares at as if
she recognizes it from something long ago.
When the potatoes are dug up, she toys with them,
tosses greens, then wolfs the dirt that clings,
or at least smudges her lips, stained like a woman's.
She lets the garden hose water her shoes, goes
bald the moment bath water touches her few thin,
blond hairs, laughs as I taught her months ago,
like a monster whose throat will hurt come morning.
She takes spills on slick grass, knocks her head
against table knobs, falls against porcelain tub walls

when the floor is wet from showers she's pulled
the curtain on. After a ten count, she returns from
her imminent bouts with swelling, bruises, and shiners
looking for more square feet, more pages to tear
loose, more and more ways to give her parents
grief and the lost sense of guiltless pleasures.

Russian Child, Nesting Doll

Just two months after I read about one couple
beating their child on the flight from Russia,
using combs, their hands, the in-flight magazine,
a week after one mother was found guilty of
shaking hers to death, the video arrived of
our Russian baby, the child I had felt as close to
as the pagan babies I bought in grammar school
and named and could never imagine, could never see.
Our daughter, who is affectionate for the camera,
who smiles, who at nine months is preparing
to crawl, is waiting, surrounded by her
undernourishment, by the electric cord that runs
just above her station or cubicle or slot,
certainly not a bed. She waits without having seen
a video of our bodies, or consulted a physician
about the circumference of our heads,
and she has no idea if we are off the charts,
or which chart a parent should be measured on.
And so we trust in randomness and those around her—
please love her, and lift her from time to time,
and share the food justly—and we prepare
the visas, the health forms, the certified
and apostilled documents, the checkbook,
enjoy our advantage of watching her again and again
respond to her name, and wake from her nap,
and buck a bit as she kneels on her pad, the way
others see the ultrasound on the screen
that one time, the wand and lubricant across
the belly revealing the kicks and arguments to come,
the unsettling of every routine, the loss of
more control, the arrival of that self you did not know
you had, or acknowledged only in private—
the statistician of error ("how many times
do I have to tell you?"), the anti-logician

of discipline and punish, the keeper of
the deep chest of lies and imperfections that are
the self. And so Marina—her given name—
Marina, wait for us as we are waiting for you.
Don't be misled by our reticence: Our love for you
is so carefully folded and pocketed and hidden
just in case you should disappear from
the Russian record books suddenly, or the country
close to foreign penetration, or the whole thing—
referrals, home-studies, references—prove a sham
as they all have seemed. Trust us, we mean
more than well. We'll fly to you, we'll take you
from those who have kept watch over you,
and we'll bring you to our home
and teach you this little we know: Our love is
flawed, chipped from use, seared from waiting,
and it is yours, our Russian child inside the child
we have been expecting, inside the child
we thought we would never have.

Near Lissadell

". . . no enemy but time."
—W.B. Yeats

My wife is in a silk kimono,
the light kind of bouncy off
the snow: she does look, oddly,
like a gazelle—all leg and limb,
her hair up in something French.
She bends—in glimmer and sheen—
to strike a match and send the news up
in flames to catch the kindling and wood.
That's cozy, she says. I wouldn't
disagree, the children conked out
in their room, the alcohol giving
even my knees some *joie de vivre*—
I feel some air under the kneecaps—
and then, what with the wine and heat
and our age, we just nod apace, wake
to needle the other with one
of the day's complaints writ small, check
the time—the kids will be up by six—
and give in, bit by bit, to what
the body stripped of politics
and vows might want: ourselves alone—
sinn fein—beneath her kimono,
inside my trousers, the fingers
that count finding each other out,
the "this again" that marrieds know well—
the neck aflame, the tongue, then the silk
hiked up, the knowledge as we climb up
each other. This is our earth, our plot,
our sphere of influence, mundane,
mondial, not rising to any other plane.

48

Above Tree Line

My wife jokes in an acidic way about her desire
to have her ashes strewn against some rock slab or
pickaxed glacial tongue, and my inability
to climb above tree line, or even up a tree,
these hip and knee joints chronically pathetic,
and worsening since I was unable to carry her
over the threshold, and she as toned as a limb.
So we barely imagine the heat of the oven and
the baking at such a high degree, the body not
anyone's anymore, or perhaps only the technician's
who, through the glass, this time watches the body
char and become boxed, ready for shipping into
the wind's heady whim. She seems to avoid thoughts
of my buried decomposition, more intent finally
on the button-down collar's missing button, and moneys
stowed for retirement's decline. After we tax
our daughter with last requests to pick up the strewn
naked dolls and Post-It notes she's drawn her
nonesuches on, and hit her with the final verse
of This Little Girl Falls Asleep Right Now
and it takes, we just hanker for our own tousled bed
and sip at drinks that clink with shining ice
and the corn fields of bourbon, and finally flub around
in the paroxysms of pleasure, loaning ourselves
from one realm of the body to another, then back
to final thoughts on some cash-fetching plan
my wife's hatched up, before she takes that last nestle
into the unflattened midsection of me, like a large child
I carry up into the skies of dream, of free-falling.

Family

When I head out the screen door into the moist
night air to empty the green Hefty trash
into the city's container I'll wheel out
come Sunday, I'm overcome (is that too large
a word?) not so much by the week's odors
or the stale and vibrant interstate arpeggio,
but by the sky high above the smell and sound,
my five-minute link with God's empty hand
three, sometimes four times a week. Today,
just past sundown, I stood while what was inside
went on without me, happier perhaps, and just
waited the birds out, the last cheep of
the cardinal, the last bravado of the mockingbird
I envied and wanted to become, as if
myth still did exist, and then in that moment
when silence finally settles in the trees—
bird romancing and skirmishing over—two or three
bats raced odd laps above the yard, they zagged
like souls looking for bodies. They whipped
large ovals and jazzed-out shapes about
the yard haloed in our neighbor's fully-watted
back porch light, and in that death of the birds'
flight and sound, and in the birth of the bats'
black against the blackening sky, I knew
I should do something, return to ritual, go in to
my daughter running the rooms, her hair
like slivers of moon, so golden and aloof.
I touched the wood of the maple and river birch,
walked across the catkin-strewn yard
and heard the interstate again—such insistency,
such a pitch of drama—and knew we were all
wheeling to meet the long line of families
who came before us, who farmed and huddled

and sharpened knives to shape a god they hoped
I would believe in. When I went back to my life,
my wife and I danced to some trash our bodies enjoy,
and we lifted our daughter up and twirled her as if
she were light, as if she'd never come back to earth.

Beyond the Pleasure Principle

I stared out, asleep, into the island that was black
and Manahatta and flat, quiet as a small number,
and smelling of wild flowers still open this late,
smelling of the flat, black river that worked toward its name,
Muheakannuck, the great waters constantly in motion,
as it went deep inside itself to become an estuary,
smelling in its mixings like something awake.

I saw the east side of the island's woods brighten from
the sun getting out of the ocean, and bright tracts
of woods fell slowly, a sound at a time, into a fort
wet with resin, then into forts and homes,
into spade handles, pick handles to unearth stones
that accumulated by stories, up into a parallel with land,
until the sum was lit with trained fires.

The white air flapped into roped-up signs of employment
and fairs with venison roasts, flapping
louder as the town rose higher above aqueducts filling
and tugboat calls, into the lights
all up a single avenue that drew a grid from itself,
then everywhere lights grew
into concrete corners, turned colors, rode in automobiles,
rose in cranes that divided into high-rises
and wrote messages of wealth into the skyscrapers
until the brightness wasn't of
a woods, deer spoor, mollusk shells and a river,
but a hot range in a corner of every home,
finger-wide lighters in every smoking hand, and faces
the size of twenty workingmen lit up on signs above all traffic.

I woke from the dream into a sunrise that made work for itself,
then went inside a dull day. But I wanted to look quickly
into the town that housed me, into the homes not yet lit

for morning, everyone still flat on his back,
into the streetlights just about to go off.
And that part of me that has always wandered toward desertion
thought everything into backwards.
Everything went easily into itself:
Our homes fell back into hills and slate finds,
the rubber coating of wires in the air and cars went back into tree sap,
the tar into an accumulation of summers,
the oil streaks floating into animal legs,
the smell of wind-pushed heat into mastodon heads melting,
and the trees that wanted only to become spring,
the simple oaks and hickories,
the simple maples and sycamores,
didn't know what they were—something spindly and green,
then something waving inside of tides,
then something just of water.

The whole town of us went under
until the earth was one steam circle,
then one hydrogen molecule waiting to turn
and become complex, and I didn't matter.
I stopped there and couldn't imagine further.
It wasn't Sunday anymore.
Breakfast wasn't a religious word.
I had nothing to pay back.
And everything in me was afraid to admit it:
I'd arrived for an instant at a thought where I wanted to belong.
The sun could part clouds and say, This way to morning!
Could tease with promises of Arousal, Vegetation, July!
But I felt from far back inside me this calling
to be where next to nothing was.

III.

The Death of the Drama Poem

Downtown, in front of the hardware store, in a moment of vision, I gave up on the prose poem and switched to the ur-drama poem. I realized those rubber hoses, the hammers, awls and potting pots I saw in the windows could be actors performing on a storefront stage. The automotive supply shop across the alley inspired me to use metaphors closer to the real world. I was able to say this:

Her hair shone like strafed mags.

I was able to say this:

His heart, a blown gasket, leaked the rich
Sentiments through.

I started to frequent many stores in my neighborhood, speaking with the owners and workers about my goals for the new genre of the drama poem, and they were taken with the idea. When business was slow the workers would toss nails in the air to imitate rain showers and twist car mirrors toward the fluorescents to make stage lights; the owners would snap their dollar bills to simulate the sounds of fists landing on a fighter's face: in this way they perfected their stage effects. Happily, I received an unsolicited grant from the Idaho Arts Council and was able to forget my job at the Ferris wheel and begin writing lines for the parts to cars, the wrenches, the mechanics with hands the color of asparagus, and even for the clientele of the Ace Hardware Store. One woman, Mrs. Di Doni, who came twice monthly to buy mousetraps, was given a few lines to recite. One week she was able to say this:

Rich man,
the mouth of heaven ain't toothless,
mark ye well.

57

Another week this:

> For the shoeshine man's funeral
> we marched slowly as a dark hill
> dragging flowers.

    This concept was expanded, first by using Mrs. Di Doni's
immediate family as the actors, and then by employing any
shopper who owned a major credit card. Customers came
from miles around to shop and recite. Then the airlines and fast
food chains transformed me into an artistic entrepreneur
when they asked me to write for them. Naturally the executives
from multinationals were not far behind.
Critics, both cultural and literary, have labeled my idea for the
fast food store a "consummate leap of the imagination,"
for there I introduced dialogue into the drama poem. Now as
the customer entered the store he would be given a drama _
poem to fit his individual needs, and the employee would then
respond with another of my creations. I wrote this for
AL'S TOWERING LOIN OF PIZZA.

Customer: Six slices please:
             One with shag-thick cheese spread
             Wide as the equator, the other five
             Tarnished slightly with mushrooms
             Large as postcards.

Employee: That will be $8.80, sir.
             Your hat presents itself
             Like a relic
             Of a felt saint.

58

Soon I was making more money than I could use. Costs and overhead were low, so I began to donate to the arts like Sim's Alignment Store, where jacks were props for an avant-garde stage, but it was hopeless. My idea was too successful. Citizens from all over the country were writing me, asking for poems to communicate those feelings for which they were unable to find the right words. Husbands and wives, even lovers, wrote me for drama poems dealing with love and sex. This is part of the one I sent to John to recite to his lover from Tulsa:

> Oh, your nipples
> Should be covered with black stars;
> Ah, your eyes
> Sealed over with black tape.

Even priests began to make special second collections to afford drama poems for the confessional. Fr. Conner received this in both English and Latin:

> Say only two Hail Marys, my son,
> But say them the way the sea
> Says time.

My hands were full. I thought maybe no one in the world was speaking but me. A devastating feeling of solipsism filled me. I would smile at people on elevators and they would start speaking, using the expensive drama poems I had patented for uncomfortable situations. Listening to the news, I would hear that Indira Gandhi had returned to India from the grave, and her opponents had thrown poached eggs at her and stuffed the ballot boxes with rye toast, and I knew this was one of my inventions now mistranslated and garbled into newspeak.

Horribly depressed, I went to my psychiatrist and spoke for nearly the entire hour about my feelings of self-absorption and self-containment. At the end of the hour he pulled out his silver pocket watch and read what was inscribed there—one of the pithiest poems I had ever written:

Love of self
Allows for no one
Nighters.

I left the office in despair, only to hear his secretary humming a drama poem I had set to music. I was living in an eternal echo. My mind was a prisoner's solitary. I wanted the world to speak to me again so I moved to Cuba, dropped the curtain on the drama poem, and began experimenting once more with the prose poem. This is one of the first I wrote there.

IV.

The Consumers

Before driving the thousands of feet up into
the clouds, we had a light lunch with Uncle Roy, outside,
near the garage where hummingbirds colored the wall

for an instant, and in the fall he gutted the elk or deer, placing
some game steaks in the deep-freeze where they still wait,
and I thought, *I guess it's OK—I like gravy as well as*

the next guy. But then in the national park, open without
an entrance fee, this being before Memorial Day when we honor
the dead with bratwurst usually, we stopped the car

for the herd of elk—maybe fifty of them—chewing around
with their clumps of coat all smitten with the urge to fall off,
walking around without their horns as if a heretic had painted

a devil or Moses, and they scratched their rotten coats
against whatever bramble they could find to get to
the undercoat, the spring design they all leaned toward.

I said, *What a beautiful thing to drive from town and feast
only the eyes and nose on this wonder,* and I chased them
to see their thighs lope and studied their spoor I swore

could have been a deer's for all I knew and I couldn't imagine
pulling some gun from a holster or scoping down the sightline
for the head or the heart of such peculiar, attentive creatures.   65

By the time we saw the third and fourth herds, however,
and they all looked the same, their skins in the same disrepair,
that congregation of light pellets again, their eyes hooked

on whoever approached, their jaws sprawling through grass,
I said to you, *This is sort of dull.* Maybe the only way to arrive at
some moment of grace or ecstasy again would be to lower the boom

on some sorry thing and hightail it home. Then it could be like
a religion with a gut-master, the entrail-handler there dropping
the knives into the useless parts, separating the chosen food

from the ribs and fat, and the creature's soul, eaten, would settle
into a part of me. But what would I do with so many souls?
What have I done? Perhaps this is why Uncle Roy had the stroke

which seems to have taken his mind away, as if it just dropped off
like some antlers in fall. Because he now acts as if he were caught
in a myth of some sort. If you ask, *How are you feeling Uncle Roy,*

he answers, *Uncle Roy.* If you say, *Are you feeling any better,*
he says, like Echo in love with what won't come back, *Any better.*
By the third or fourth time he does this you get the idea, and he too

seems kind of unimportant or dull until he starts to cry
at inappropriate times, and although the doctors have explained
to the immediate family that this *is* a normal

and systematic physiological response by the blood-shocked head,
still his tears get the better of you and you end up
at his level, just repeating whatever it was you were taught to say

at such moments. Maybe no one should be allowed to live.
Or maybe only the saints, who punish themselves and everyone else
they know, should be awarded the license to walk around,

their hair all mangy and ridiculous, as if they knew no barber
who displayed for the waiting the monthly magazines of women
trying to twist their bodies into something individual, distinctive,

something outside the norm so men would love them and they'd
be granted some form of ecstatic life in the flesh.
Is there something so horrible about life that the only ones

worthy of it are those who hate it and want to die?
Is paradise a stream of light that, after the first few times
you see it, still retains its allure, its draw

and you feel no need for something else, something better?

What History Joined Together

I'm driving not too badly on the other side
of the road, listening to my wife explain
to my aunt, a nun from Belfast, just what
her religion is, and after a mile or two
of liturgical distinctions and farmland
up the River Bann, I make abruptly clear
that Episcopalian means Church of Ireland,
and finally my aunt yields and settles in,
until I ask her to point out where the Catholic
was shot in retaliation last week, and she
shows us the wreath and the door, blessing
herself as I do. My wife soothes our daughter,
still reeling from the time change, and I
ask my aunt to explain my cousin's ecumenical
gift for removing sties that draws believers
from miles around the farm. As she talks
the British helicopter just ahead of us
swoons, and I'm reminded of the morning
my father challenged the troops who crossed
the farm, avoiding the hollow and the moss,
and he yelled, *By what right? By whose God?*
while my cousin tried to draw him back to
the house where he was born. My aunt is the last
of that generation alive, and so when she falls
asleep in the rental and my daughter joins her,
my wife and I are left to enjoy the quiet,
the speed bumps at checkpoints, the radio news
that lets us know we don't belong. I try
to recount myths about the children of Lir,
give history lessons about Connolly and Pearse,
Thatcher's unbending blasphemy, the plantation
of my father's Ulster, but all she hopes for
is the eel's quick freedoms we glimpsed in
Lough Neagh, that glint of speed away from here

where she is almost enemy by birth. Perhaps
because she was born alongside Nebraska's
weather, not Ireland's history, she can not quite
fathom the lure, the power of tit-for-tat killing,
the centuries-long magnificat in praise of
lording it over, vanquishing, never surrendering
what has been taken, and the other side's desire
to rebel in kind, even if the rebellion almost
takes orders from a circle of hell shared by
the oppressor, where all the past's heroes lie
still mulling over both sides' rights and bones.

1920

What would I give to have been there
Forty years before you named me for a revolutionary
Hanged that November, to see you walking with your father
In winter, the soil hard and cleaned of the crops.
You were twelve and took the hills with an ash stick
That was taller than your father who still held
Your hand near the bog pits, warning you and yarning
Stories of bodies and firearms, even churns filled with butter
Buried into the thick of the blackness; things might not
Rise from the bottom with the mist in the mornings,
But solid objects stayed solid for centuries and more—
No small comfort for a boy in winter with an old father
Who would die that spring, a boy cursed and blessed
With a Catholic imagination, and with the adult talk
Of insurrection and reprisals taken in through floorboards
When he should be sleeping at night. But your father
Lifted you out of all thought and twirled you past
Bog, stacked peat, turned-up soil and farmhouse,
Your long walking stick pointing out and moving across
What the family had owned farther back than your mind
Could go. And your father told you then as your feet
Went home to the ground that you were too frail, too light
To be a farmer—"Read books, Bernard, and find
Your work in town." This is the moment I want for my own,
As the first touch of danger met you, as you saw
Yourself different from what came before, different
From father and brothers, different from the Drummuck
Hills that were your home. I want to see you grow
Into this early courage, plant the stick in the ground
And raise yourself up in its give, not trying to show
A lie to your father, not denying what your body
Would do, but standing there with all the tallness
A boy could rise up to who learned at twelve

What his future wouldn't be. And I suppose I want
To see you suffering, unsure, still wanting to hold
His hand, your mind whirling though he put you down
Some time before. I want to have this day in winter
On the farm that right then stopped being your own,
And I want you boyish and small and courageous
And swirling, because you left the farm for town,
Left Ireland finally for America, brought me into
Danger and into our troubles, and became what you are,
Providing me with my inheritance of failed rebellion.

Out of the Body

"God, she had great legs, Bernard," he says, and brings her
out from the wallet, a photo from Europe in the forties
after the war, "and she wasn't afraid to show them, huh?"
And in the photo, she sits not quite demurely, but properly
showing maybe three inches above the knees. The legs
are wonderful. "But you know, Bernard, she suffered
in silence. We drove recently from Florida to Georgia
and the whole way she doesn't say a word. We get out
of the car and the back of her dress—it was a white cotton—
was filled with blood. The tumors must have been everywhere."

All this at the wake. She's there in the room, her voice
that was deeper than Bacall's gone, the hands that lifted
drinks until the end wrapped in a rosary with beads smaller
than the age spots. The next day the soldiers will lift
the colonel's wife from the car and walk marching in step
up the hill at Arlington to let her into the ground.

"At the end, the Alzheimer's, Bernard, made her turn on everyone
she loved. It was not her there. And she wanted to die,
for months, maybe the last six she wanted to die. She loved
visiting you and your family: the mashed potatoes piled
to here and the gallons of milk. 'Now that,' she used to say,
'that's a family.'" They had no children. She perhaps
was too old. He turns mostly the good side of his face
toward us; cancer has taken the right chin and cheekbone,
and tomorrow he will not be able to walk up the hill to sit
for the military priest's final words. "The emphysema, Bernard,
the doctors say it'll kill me soon. You know, Bernard, if I
had to do it all over again I'd be a urologist and settle
in Florida. My God, the money they make. Hand over fist
into our ass, fingering for the prostate; 'swollen or not,
here we come.' She was something though, Bernard. And how's
Marge?" "Fair," my father says. "Just fair." Neither man
cries until the funeral mass when the priest says,

"Pray for her and ask her to pray for us. We will see her again, not in the body, as we once were, but changed. All of us joined again, pure spirits. This flesh transformed."

Begetter and Begotten

My father and I wore the black rubber boots
for hygiene, walked between two lines of cows—
their rumps toward us—watching for the rise
of tails, keeping clear of the concrete troughs,

the runnels of excrement and urine. Our host,
my sister's neighbor—gloved, booted, raincoated—
approached each cow to place his arm-length tube
inside of them, his other arm checking from deep

inside the proper location by feel, by touch.
He placed the bull sperm inside the six to a side,
returned the dry-ice baskets to the truck, snapped
off the elbow-length gloves, signed logs,

gave us the odds for conception his company offered,
and walked us past the slicks of ice to our car.
He slapped the roof to send us off the way
he slapped cowhide. On the low road back to my sister's,

my father spoke again after four days of chit-chat
about final judgment—the transition from
chilled sperm to God not greased. He reasoned
with passion that belief should not break off here

in America after our church had endured more than
four hundred years of oppression in Ireland.
His hands looked for metaphors as he gestured
toward the landscape, the cold ground, and he said,

"I love the look of cows, from haunches to hooves,
but they are dumb to all this. Don't you think about
the end of all you love, your mother's death and mine
and yours? Do you think of your body after death,

as good to you as pickled pig feet are to the dead hog?"
He stopped to warn about my speeding, my one hand
on the wheel, then waited for some response, but I
had been taught, when young, not to argue. I was more

silent than the sky. Besides, my position was weak.
I was driving my father on what he jokingly called
his "Farewell Tour," his last visit at eighty-eight
to his children's homes, driving through New England

back to Philadelphia where his plot sits
and my mother's sits, and mine, there for years now, looking
out onto the expressway that crosses the river, bought
so the children would have one less thing to deal with.

Before Bed

After unsnapping the garters and slipping the stockings
off, helping the slip off after the dress, over the head,
and lifting the six hooks from their eyes on my side,
I remove and fold the girdle while she gets the panties
down and works the front-hooking bra loose.
I sift for the nightgown in the pile of hose and girdles
in the chair she leans on before she walks awkwardly toward
the toilet. Then I go to the other single bed and help
my father off with his shoes and socks, and dress
the long wound again, then help my mother swing
into bed, like something heavy that is turning on a bad
bearing. I say goodnight, and kiss, and turn out the lights
and hear them immediately talk—what my father always called
a mouthful of prayers—the call and response fading as I
walk downstairs. My father always calls and before my mother
can finish, my father calls again. In the Hail Mary
he is the Angel Gabriel and my mother is the very human,
anonymous soul asking for thoughtfulness, for kindness
at the hour of death—not the moment, because the event is long.

Waking

I help my mother on the toilet, I help her off,
her cotton housedress soaked through with sweat,
and so I take it off with her undershirt and bra.
I place the white, round pill and the fuchsia square
on her tongue and hold the glass as she shakes
and sucks at the straw. I let her rest
beneath the sheet, naked, the industrial fan
in the hall on airplane-high. At fourteen,
I watched her in the mirror in her slip bend
for the lower dresser drawer while I pretended
to sleep, but watched, the fullness, the firmness,
her body once mine, all hers. I do not recognize it
now in her diminishment, her thirteenth year
of worsening, of sickness, her tremors
so strong the bed shakes and groans, her hands
unable to turn the TV's remote on to watch
Wheel of Fortune and then *Jeopardy,* and so I do
her that favor, and turn the lights off and kiss
her dry lips, touch her sweat-darkened hair,
unable sometimes to accept her lack of a death-wish,
her happiness when morning comes, the TV still on.
Her tremors are gone for now, and the awful ache
in the spine and hips and feet and head
and wrists. In that moment of peace before
the next rack of pains, she's thankful, serene,
happy to touch my hand, to hold her cane, to sit up
for the breakfast in bed: prune juice, bran, coffee
and grapes she hardly touches. Her mind is going
where her body leads her, not knowing this day
of pain from the next, and in that loose skein
of thought she seems almost content, almost gone.

In Heat

—for Bridget and E. J.

The summer heats past luxuriance, the day lilies
flower after the poppies expire, their milk brimming
around the seed. The cherries turn red as
the bird beaks clean them to pits that just
hang—until winds come—too naked on the stem.
Like the busy woman at the pool with a suit
that announced her nipples—circle, circle—
too loudly when your friend beside you with
the mastectomy has been speaking of having
an areola tattooed to what's left.

The deer, in pairs like Mormons on mission through
these streets, lift heads from lettuce or thyme
as you drive past, the street like buckshot for them.
The creek that runs like a river is filling still
against the sandbagged walls, the melting from winter
still finishing, still working back to stone,
to the naked speech of granite, that bluntness.

When the sun goes down just past solstice, sprinklers
that are timed spout as the drizzle arrives.
Sirens announce a tornado touching down nearby
just as cloud-to-cloud lightning ricochets briefly,
its heat stronger than the sun's which will rise again
soon. So those with money wedge themselves into
lines for ice cream after dark, or drink until
their heads feel like hedgehogs' asleep. And some
just work past the sweat and find in the simplest
sounds that bodies make—whether the slap of father
to child, or the tongue-love of soon-to-be separated
lovers—a place to camp, to wait it out, to allow
the sun's slow wane, its ticking toward equinox.

Just someplace not so close to here where the heat
makes the catamarans up on bricks and beneath tarp
look like entrapment, and the shotgun—or at least
those barrels, so clean and cloudlike—seems like
a confidante, the lover you finally find who can
listen closely to the most private things and
those little black eyes don't flinch. Just fire.

Masturbating on Ash Wednesday

I didn't know I WAS in fact until the next day's news
with photographs of children with ashen smudges
on their foreheads, not the nicely done cross as in my day—
rush, rush. I only knew I had spent a week with my parents,
changing them after their accidents, helping them on and off
toilets, helping them dress and undress—my father always
cold, despite the long underwear, my mother always warm, sweating.
I tried to answer all my mother's questions: *Where am I exactly?*
What kind of a place is this? Why are those wires in the wall?
When I passed the baton on to a sibling, I flew away
from my father reciting his half of the decade of the rosary
as my mother's mind leapt from cloud to cloud in her sleep.
So much misery, and paralysis, and gradual dimming,
that when my Web search took me off target
onto photographs of TEENS NEVER BEFORE SEEN NAKED, and they
        seemed
so content, so pleasantly desirous, so at peace with the flesh,
so oblivious in their nakedness of the next step, or page, or search,
I fell into that glorious enlargement and hands-on approach
to the denial of the body's slow effacement, its on-deck erasure.
This way I ignore it just long enough to find the pleasures,
forgetting for a time the inevitable loosening of controls
of bladder, of mind, of gesture, of tongue,
placing the cursor right on those bodies—so full, so distant,
so amply poised, so twined with the fall.

Excision

—for Barbara

Raised Catholic, daughter of Bellagamba
and Giordano, she has moved to a diet free
from anything with a face and to Zen,
but paging through art one night without nausea,

in the sixth day of radiation, after discovery
and chemo, after the scarves and near veils, she sees
the painting of Saint Agatha holding her own severed
breasts on the pewter plate, like John the Baptist's head,

and reads the commentary on the cruelty of
metaphor, how the Sicilian martyr became
patron saint to bakers whose loaves must rise
and to bell-founders. She fingers the skin-site

where lump and flesh around the lump were lifted
from her and placed on the surgical tray, doesn't
turn the page, doesn't think through, doesn't
doze this time. She closes the book on her finger

and believes for a moment she sees a Christ
behind the French doors, in the guest room
with the African masks and three cats whose fur
bristles and then sparks in radiance at His touch.

Death Doesn't Occur

Even in a large family death doesn't occur
every day, so when our dog died that walked on
twos to beg, or got the belt for chewing
the stuff that chair seats are made of
or the woodwork edges while we were at church,
my mother cried as I haven't seen often, perhaps
not even when her mother died who had seen
Buffalo Bill and Sitting Bull in Manhattan and
thugs with gun butts in her seventh story walk-up
in the Bronx, the last white woman in her complex,
she'd proudly announce, as if poverty were a prize.
My mother does report when her children cry—calling
home with their cancer scares and biopsies,
the uterus and spleen removals, her daughter's
tubal occlusions that'll prevent any children, or
her son's loss of his child who died at two
with a diseased bowel. But she hardly cries herself,
except when my father at eighty-six had his bypass
and she wondered what would become of her. Because
what has become of her has not been good: Parkinson's,
spinal stenosis, false hips and somewhat repaired
vertebrae, arthritis in every joint known to God,
skin cancer in her face, a memory that has scratches
in its surface, feet that swell and ankles that pain her
even as she rises up the stairs in her electric stairlift.
Her upper lip is stiff from the years,
but she feels more than I ever have. She blesses
herself still when ambulances pass, their sirens lit,
she prays after the news at six, she hopes for
the resurrection of the dead because she misses
the lot of them. And she laughs still. There is something
almost joyously primitive about her when she comes to
the punch line of some story or joke. And when she laughs
that hard her hands will approach her mouth

to cover it so quickly her muscles will cramp
in the bicep, and she or I or someone there—is anyone
there?—will rub it until the part that is hard
relaxes into its flaccid self. She'll thank God
it didn't get worse, her skin sweating from the girdle
that holds her back up, her head twisting from
the Parkinson's, and she'll say, *Thank God the cramp passed.*
Not a tear in her eye. The woman is almost a God
looking down on her own pain. She must find it remarkable.

Catechize

I thought I would feel an erasure or
some sort of consolation if
I found the source of the wrist-wide runnel,
deeper than wide—that if I tracked it
back through the reeds and grass still humble
in March and learned something, I could
remember that later when I was alone inside.
I stopped for the tree's fungus, the rotting
altar that, when mature, can hold writing, but
now was too soft. And stopped for a weighing,
my first, of a single deer spoor. It must be
hollow or made of straw, it's that light
and redolent of nothing. Spiders walked
above, or leapt faster than, the current
I walked against, up toward the road and line
of mailboxes—seven in red with arms up
at angles to signal. Fastened to a hedge
of bramble, a nest with gum wrapper stood out,
empty, disadvantaged, and ahead of it,
where the four hills that are mounds
naturally give up and lie down, there
the creek had two sources—a lake of
stagnation, filmed with living sediment,
wide as a cow, a circle, and beside it,
a tribute to unchecked license, a spring
surface I think, something that took
a branch's poking about a foot or two
back past itself, unanswerable. I played
with the word origin, remembering the Father
of the Church who, in Alexandria, in youth
and steady conviction, made himself a eunuch
for the kingdom's sake, slicing his testicles
off to cease the wrestle, to align himself

closer with the stars he thought could sin
less. He came out of it certain, healing,
washing away the several known sins
and finding around himself all that covets
and ravens the soul and has breath.
I stuck my fingers up to the knuckles in
the soil by the pool; it was moist, hospitable.
Then I raised them, smelled them.
What creation in that rot. What a smell—
dark, with the weight of a river.

Recall

In reading Celan who drowned in the Seine—
a suicide—I begin to remember this German
I've studied and forgotten, like so many things:
constellations, the calls of birds, the faces
of those who have died, the taste of
their lips. And I enjoy these words: *Sanduhr*—
sand hour—is their hourglass. On the beach
you can hear the sounds from the womb if
you let sand fall through your hand. Celan's mother
was shot in the neck in an internment camp.
Pubic hair is *Schamhaar*—shame hair. He was born
in Czernowitz, last name Antschel, then Ancel, then
—in an anagram—Celan, adopted after his father's death
from typhus in the camps. *Auschwitz* is so close
to sweat out, *Buchenwald* is beech woods. *Kraut*
is herb or plant. His first son died in infancy.
Augapfel—eyeball—is literally eye apple—apple
of the eye. The child died. Sex is *Geschlecht*—
schlecht being bad, rotten. *Heidekraut* is heather.
My father cannot speak well anymore. He slurs,
drunkenly, from the stroke, from the lacunar infarctions,
the doctor says. *Sarg* is coffin, perhaps like our
sarcophagus—Greek for flesh eater. Oblivion is
Vergessen and to forget is *vergessen*. *Essen* is
to eat. The earth eats us. In Greece, they placed
coins in the mouths of the dead for Charon's payment.
Lip is *Lippe*, red *rot*, blood *Blut*, and urn *Urn*.
Take the words from the dead, the dying, and change
them, God. Change them. Let the words say clearly,
Life is good. Life is good. *Alles ist in Ordnung.*

Legerdemain

It was a Campbell, a great aunt, who was laid
out on ice the way they did then, then rose again
from her own wake in her own home. *For the love
of Christ, get me out of here,* she said. *I'm freezing
my ass off.* This was a story we could believe in
when we couldn't believe the other one about Christ.
No one expected the same legerdemain with
my father, down for the count, dead at ninety-five,
but my mother still turns heads now when she
asks him what he's doing, and says, *Don't dilly-dally,
come sit down, this isn't bad this time,* speaking of
the noodles and sauce. Or in the morning,
when her mind is freshest, she'll ask,
*Did you get it straightened out with Dad
last night?* And I'll lower my head the way I did
to lie about mass or some sacrament I owed
something to, and say, *Yes, yes I did, Mom.*
And then I'll ask her to grip the bedrail and roll
slightly so we can wash this here and now,
apply the gel to her backside, the bedsore
healing now, no longer like a sick peach, some
damaged skin you'd show to the doctor and ask,
Is this something to be worried about?
She says, *I'm fine, don't worry about me. Look
To your father there. Is that him there?*
Yes, yes it is, back from the crypt, back from
the inching down, the striped suit and the gold tooth,
(did they leave the gold tooth in, the shysters?)
and the well polished shoes with cleats.
The pants' crease still pressed, the spit-shine
all glow, the cleats nailed in, the moustache
so finely trimmed. That's all of him.

Oneness

On the fifth night of high seas, the cattle and fowl and creeping things
cried out through the pitch, rolled and clawed in an exchange of floor
    space,
huddled into the port section, then turned to other wards of the slaver,
while in the fore-cabin, not in the hull, but separate and better,
flooded in light from rendered fat, with wine falling and heading into
    streams,
Noah approached his wife and said:

"Although, since we left the land, we have neither seen nor heard
any of our animals mate, perhaps because they are without the earth
    beneath them,
we should because the land is in our minds,
and that vial of soil you wisely stowed aboard holds all the sanctity we
    need.
Let's, my chosen one, wring to fulfillment our lust together.
You are not my sister—though I wanted you to be.
You are not my mother—though I wanted you to be.
You are no one to me but someone I love outside my blood."

As he remembered in his memory good for numbers and facts,
the gnats and cattle and snakes and crickets and fowl and apes—
the apes were in the square cages safely below—bringing themselves
    to the other,
he approached his wife, his hair a sight, his pallor a shame,
his tongue fat with the fruit of the vine, and his schlong fat with the
    same,
and he began in a reminiscent way to unlock the belts around his
    wife's waist
and splay her legs to let his way with her begin.

Below, animal tails were rising, the fear of the seas
unsettling their routines, and they heard from upstairs, above, on high
the sounds of master and maid—his voice of "desist" and "again"
    they'd know anywhere.

They tried to stand their ground and learn from his ways,
but now with the stench of stabled excrement, the random waves,
the rotting grains, small comfort was theirs
without the earth beneath their feet or pads or abdomens or brains.
Just the gopher wood already splintering and clawed through.
But they were quiet. And heard her say:

"Noah, no, Noah, no, Noah, put me back. I am not the woman your
    mind thinks.
In spirit I have not been your wife for seven days, my six hundred-year-
    old man.
Most of what I was is beneath the waters now with those we loved."

Then he whispered in ecstasy nearly:

"It's all the same. We're all the same.
You're the same. It's all the same.
I love you just the same. You're the same."

The Heart of It

Pyramid of the sun, pyramid of the moon,
pre-Aztec ruins, we're on our way there
when the guide announces our luck: weavings,
the most beautiful metalwork, hand-etched obsidian masks,
shelves of artisanry, will be our next stop.
Unannounced before, but planned, and so
we disembark, the *muchacho* from Panama,
the woman from Vera Cruz with a daughter
in her wallet, and the round man from Brazil
who was born in Chile. I have joined
an international team to learn at this *tienda*
of the most authentic copies of the pyramids
embossed on tablecloths made from the fiber
of the agave plant that also yields from its heart—
beneficent—tequila, mescal, and pulque we can test
in Dixie-cup shots, first mescal with its worm
for *sabor,* then tequila straight up, then mescal
and pulque and tequila, the foursome soon chanting,
arriba, abajo, al centro, y pa' dentro!! I am in
a fraternity now, learning the drinking songs
in a cross-cultural way, celebrating the diversity
of blood laced with straight sun and alcohol.
And then Ernesto, our local guide, says, *We do have*
time to shop, and whether it is the little waves
on the worm's body like a screw's, or the halter
on the woman from Vera Cruz—a false cross between
her breasts, bodiless, all wood—or the stacked goods
like the stacked homes we turned away from in the van,
each the color of sand painted with rain,
we do commence shopping for earrings with gods
hanging, pendant, and shirts sporting heads and tails
of Quetzalcoatl, or the little pronged corn holders
inlaid with fake marble we all buy up, returning
for the aqua vitae whenever we care to. I have never

bought so much in a single standing, the cloth and
clothes and scarves and rings and temples I can cup
in my two hands, oh pyramid scheme I enjoy so, almost
hugging the boy from Panama who confides a love
for Michael Jordan still and his disgraced Bulls,
or the Brazilian who calls his whore back in town,
letting me speak with her briefly on his cell: I say
over and over, as if it were love's true word, *Cómo? Cómo?*
Then we wane into our van seats for the short ride
to the pyramid whose steep steps we'll climb to the peak.
The woman from Vera Cruz suffers from stitches in her side
and dry heaves, the boy almost soars as he races up
and back up again, but is met at the gate because
his purchases were nixed in a credit card check,
and the man from Brazil, from the flat top of
the pyramid of the sun, dials his whore again, and says,
"I love you even more now that I am at the top of the world,
mi amor," hangs up, smiles and says, "She is a great fuck, *señor*".

Hollowed

—on the 25th anniversary of the Woodstock summer

They came, half a million strong, out of
Rwanda, into Zaire, into Tanzania, half
a million in half a day, then another million
the next. They came to a land without trees,
without crops, to water soon fouled.
The sounds of voices, more moans than song, rose
from the ground the corpses lay on.
Women and men covered their faces with cloth,
each body, even in death, giving off
its own individual smell, its degree of rot.
The government had been reborn out of ashes
and macheted torsos. The cholera nestled,
stirred, profited. It danced inside, brought on
the diarrhea, and passed from this body to
that body of water, stained it, ruined it for
others to drink. Some took the Red Cross needles
of salts and fluids into their arms and then
died. Others died on their own, on their piece
of the ground, their bodies emptied, hollowed.
The crowds of dying were well behaved. Two million
would be content with a carapace for shelter,
with some god's spoiled manna or some roots.
When supplies arrived from airfields by truck,
the throng rushed the truck beds as only the dying can,
and held their arms out, or stood for
as long as they could, until the stars circled,
until the morning when the sun warmed them again
and they ate and then died. And some who lived
returned to hear the hacking sounds of their
nation's anthem. Some bodies coursed the river,
at one with sticks, cans, eddies, logs.

Our Last Child's First Day of School

When we slip right into sleep, the way smooth
Like sheen from drink, we call that a nocturnal omission.
And when I slid right down from your face to half-mast,
We said I was going down under, and this was Australia,
Equipped with kiwi hair, and this little island
A Zealand, old as the earth and eternal. But
Mostly we perform the paces of parenthood, moving
What was there back to back there, whether
It's some white doll that looks like trash, or the soiled
Undies flowery enough to wear for three days,
Or the pendulum movement of emptying the dishes
From our sacred dishwasher, that diurnal tick-tock
That grates so. Everything is repetition, from
The snarl of disobedience, to eating the forbidden candy,
To the tormenting of one child by the other,
Until last week on our daughter's first day of school
We repaired to the room we're stripping
The paint off and caulking the cracks in,
And there amid the lucky ladder with spread legs just so,
The gentle hair of the paint brush, and the lost
Power Puff Girl maze, we found our way back to bed
And what started this whole thing, that bending without pain,
That startling invention of fingernails, skin
Alert, interested in everything that's going on
And in, focused, one thing at a time,
And then everything at once.

photo by Tess Boyle

Kevin Boyle was born and grew up in Philadelphia, receiving his
B.A. from the University of Pennsylvania. He attended graduate
school at Boston University and the University of Iowa. His
poems have appeared in a number of magazines, including
*Alaska Quarterly, Colorado Review, Denver Quarterly, Greensboro
Review, Michigan Quarterly Review, North American Review,
Northwest Review, Poet Lore, Poetry East,* and *Virginia Quarterly
Review.* His chapbook, *The Lullaby of History,* won the Mary Belle
Campbell Poetry Book Prize and was published in 2002. Boyle
teaches at Elon University in North Carolina, where he lives with
his wife and two daughters.

New Issues Poetry & Prose

Editor, Herbert Scott

Vito Aiuto, *Self-Portrait as Jerry Quarry*
James Armstrong, *Monument in a Summer Hat*
Claire Bateman, *Clumsy*
Maria Beig, *Hermine: An Animal Life* (fiction)
Kevin Boyle, *A Home for Wayward Girls*
Michael Burkard, *Pennsylvania Collection Agency*
Christopher Bursk, *Ovid at Fifteen*
Anthony Butts, *Fifth Season*
Anthony Butts, *Little Low Heaven*
Kevin Cantwell, *Something Black in the Green Part of Your Eye*
Gladys Cardiff, *A Bare Unpainted Table*
Kevin Clark, *In the Evening of No Warning*
Cynie Cory, *American Girl*
Peter Covino, *Cut Off the Ears of Winter*
Jim Daniels, *Night with Drive-By Shooting Stars*
Joseph Featherstone, *Brace's Cove*
Lisa Fishman, *The Deep Heart's Core Is a Suitcase*
Robert Grunst, *The Smallest Bird in North America*
Paul Guest, *The Resurrection of the Body and the Ruin of the World*
Robert Haight, *Emergences and Spinner Falls*
Mark Halperin, *Time as Distance*
Myronn Hardy, *Approaching the Center*
Brian Henry, *Graft*
Edward Haworth Hoeppner, *Rain Through High Windows*
Cynthia Hogue, *Flux*
Christine Hume, *Alaskaphrenia*
Janet Kauffman, *Rot* (fiction)
Josie Kearns, *New Numbers*
David Keplinger, *The Clearing*
Maurice Kilwein Guevara, *Autobiography of So-and-So: Poems in Prose*
Ruth Ellen Kocher, *When the Moon Knows You're Wandering*